RESPONSIBLE PARENTING

How to raise a responsible and a happy family

Stephen William

Dedication

This book is dedicated to parent, guidance and single who intend to build or raise a family.

Table of content

PRACTICAL TIPS FOR BE A RESPONSIBLE PARENT

Introduction

Being a parent is one of the most challenging yet profitable roles in life. It's an adventure complete of United States and downs, joys and challenges, and it calls for a variety of duty. As a determine, you're accountable for shaping the lifestyles of another individual, and that is no small assignment. In state-of-the-art international, elevating an infant has grown to be greater tough than ever before, with so many distractions and competing priorities. So how do you make certain that you are being a responsible parent? In this post, we've compiled some practical tips to help you navigate the adventure of parenthood with confidence and simplicity. From setting limitations to leading with the aid of instance, these suggestions will assist you prioritize your infant's needs and ensure that you are being the nice figure you may be.

Lead by instance

As a determine, you're the maximum influential function version in your baby's lifestyles. Children analyze through observing and imitating the behavior of these round them, so it's critical that you lead by means of example. If you want your infant to develop right habits, then you definitely need to exhibit them yourself.

For instance, in case you need your baby to be honest, then you should always be honest with them. If you want your baby to have top manners, then you definitely must display courtesy and politeness to others. If you need your toddler to be bodily active, then you need to interact in regular workout yourself.

It's crucial to remember the fact that kids are usually looking and listening, even when you assume they are now not paying interest. So, consider of your actions and conduct always. Set a nice instance and your baby could be much more likely to follow in your footsteps.

Leading by instance no longer best teaches your child critical values and ideas, however it additionally facilitates to construct a strong and trusting relationship between you and your child. So, ensure you are placing a great example to your toddler to follow.

Set clear expectations and limitations

Setting clean expectations and limitations is an vital part of being a accountable figure. Children need structure and consistency on the way to sense cozy and increase a experience of obligation themselves.

It's crucial to communicate your expectations genuinely on your toddler and make certain they apprehend what is predicted of them. This consists of such things as policies around behavior, chores, homework and curfews. When kids recognize what's anticipated of them, they may be much more likely to satisfy those expectancies.

Boundaries are also crucial. Children want to realize what's and isn't always perfect conduct. This consists of physical obstacles, along with respecting non-public space, as well as emotional obstacles, which includes respecting every other's feelings.

As a accountable discern, it is vital to set obstacles which can be suitable for your toddler's age and development level. You should also be steady in imposing these obstacles, and ensure that consequences for breaking them are honest and consistent.

When setting expectations and boundaries, it's important to be firm however honest. Listen on your toddler's issues and be willing to make adjustments if essential. By putting clear expectations and limitations, you can help your toddler expand a feel of obligation, and create a effective and supportive environment for their increase and improvement.

Practice active listening

One of the maximum crucial elements of being a responsible figure is to exercise active listening. Active listening is the artwork of truly listening to what your toddler is announcing and responding in a way that suggests that you understand and care about their emotions.

As parents, it is simple to fall into the trap of thinking that we usually recognize what is satisfactory for our kids, however this could often lead to misunderstandings and a lack of believe within the determine-baby dating.

By practicing energetic listening, we are able to benefit a higher know-how of our baby's want and desires, and build a stronger bond of accept as true with and communiqué.

Active listening includes giving our toddler our full interest whilst they're speaker to us. This way placing away distractions which include phones or the television, and making eye contact with our toddler when they're talking. We need to also try to avoid interrupting or brushing off our child's mind and emotions, and instead inspire them to specific themselves fully.

By displaying that we're absolutely being attentive to our child, we can help them to feel valued and revered, and construct a more potent, greater information courting.

Active listening is a simple but effective device for any accountable discern, and may assist to create a satisfied and healthful own family dynamic.

Show love and affection

Showing love and affection is one of the cornerstones of accountable parenting. Children who experience loved and valued grow as much as be more confident and properly-adjusted adults. As a discern, you may display love and affection to your baby in lots of methods. Here are some examples:

1. <u>Hug your baby regularly:</u> Physical touch is a powerful manner to expose love and

affection. Hugging your toddler often, in particular while they may be feeling unhappy or dissatisfied, can assist them experience comforted and reassured.

2. <u>Use phrases of confirmation:</u> Tell your toddler how a lot you adore them and how proud you're of them. Praise them for their accomplishments and encourage them when they're struggling.

3. <u>Spend high-quality time collectively:</u> Make time to do things along with your infant that they revel in. This could be something from playing a recreation to

going for a walk to looking a film collectively.

4. <u>Listen for your infant:</u> When your baby wants to talk to you, supply them your complete attention. Listen to what they have to mention and reply with empathy and know-how.

5. <u>Show physical affection:</u> In addition to hugs, you could also show bodily affection by way of conserving your child's hand, giving them a pat on the returned, or maybe just sitting close to them on the couch.

By displaying love and affection for your child, you are supporting them increase a strong experience of self-esteem and a deep connection with you. This will not best benefit them inside the gift however additionally inside the future as they navigate their manner through life.

Teach respect and obligation

One of the most important obligations of being a discern is coaching your baby admire and duty. This is a crucial thing in their development as it allows them to navigate the arena and have interaction with others in a nice way. Teaching admires and responsibility is going past just telling your child what to do; it includes main through instance and creating an environment in which these values are continually reinforced.

Start by placing clean expectations and barriers to your toddler. This includes guidelines around behavior, chores, and homework. Make sure your baby knows why these guidelines are essential and the consequences of not following them. Consistency is key in terms of parenting, so make sure you put in force these policies constantly.

Teaching obligation also way giving your infant age-appropriate responsibilities and responsibilities. This could be as easy as making their mattress within the morning, or more complex responsibilities like cleaning the toilet or doing the grocery buying. Giving your toddler these duties now not handiest teaches them critical existence abilities, however additionally instills a experience of satisfaction and accomplishment.

Finally, coaching admire includes modeling respectful behavior yourself. This manner treating your baby, and others, with kindness and empathy. It also approaches being respectful of various viewpoints and critiques, and teaching your infant to do the identical.

In quick, teaching admire and duty is a important a part of being a accountable discern. By setting clear expectancies, giving your toddler responsibilities, and modeling respectful behavior, you can assist your infant navigate the arena in a superb and meaningful way.

Encourage independence

Encouraging independence is a vital thing of responsible parenting. It is vital to present youngsters the liberty and possibilities to research and develop on their own. Children who develop a experience of independence are more likely to come to be self-enough and assured adults.

As a determine, it is crucial to begin small and progressively growth duties as the child grows older. For example, more youthful children can be endorsed to get dressed themselves, Their personal college bag, or assist with simple family chores. As they become older, they may be given more obligations consisting of managing their personal finances, planning their own schedules, and making their own selections.

It's critical to be aware tat encouraging independence does not suggest neglecting your baby. It actually means allowing them to examine from their errors and letting them take ownership of their lives. As a figure, it is essential to find a stability among being supportive and allowing your child to take the lead.

By encouraging independence, you're coaching your baby valuable existence abilities and constructing their confidence. This will not most effective gain them in their adolescence but additionally throughout their adult life.

Foster open communication

One of the most vital matters you can do as a accountable figure is to foster open conversation together with your children. Children want to sense comfy and safe speaking to their dad and mom about whatever and everything. As a parent, it is your obligation to create an environment that encourages open conversation.

Make time to speak with your youngsters on a regular basis. Ask them about their day, their thoughts, and their feelings. Listen to them closely and with out judgment, and allow them to understand which you are usually to be had to talk. Encourage them to ask questions and proportion their issues with you.

When your children do come to you with a hassle or a query, make an effort to actually listen to them. Avoid interrupting or leaping to conclusions. Instead, ask questions and try to apprehend their perspective. This will help your child feel heard and revered, and could make stronger your dating with them.

Remember that open verbal exchange is a - manner street. It's crucial to proportion your mind and emotions with your children as well. Be honest and open with them, and allow them to recognize that they are able to continually come to you for advice and assist. By fostering open communiqué, you may create a stronger bond with your youngsters with a view to remaining a life-time.

Promote a healthy way of life

Promoting a healthy way of life in your children is vital to their increase and improvement. Encouraging healthy conduct from a young age can set them up for a lifetime of good fitness.

One of the maximum crucial methods to sell a wholesome life-style is via encouraging bodily hobby. Make positive your kids get enough exercising each day, whether it's thru prepared sports, gambling outside, or simply going for a stroll or motorcycle experience. Limiting screen time and inspiring outdoor play is likewise beneficial for his or her physical fitness.

In addition to bodily interest, it is crucial to sell wholesome eating habits. Make certain your children have get right of entry to to nutritious meals and snacks, and restriction sugary or processed meals. Encourage them to attempt new fruits and veggies and contain them in meal making plans and education.

Ensuring your kids get enough sleep is likewise vital for his or her normal health. Establish a regular bedtime ordinary and restriction screen time before bed to sell top sleep habits.

By promoting a healthful life-style for your kids, you aren't only putting them up for exact physical fitness but additionally encouraging high-quality conduct and behaviors as a way to benefit them at some point of their lives.

Provide safe and nurturing surroundings

As a responsible parent, it is crucial to provide a secure and nurturing environment for your toddler. This way making sure that your home is secure, comfortable, and unfastened from any dangers that could harm your child. You can begin by means of infant-proofing your home, installing baby-protection locks on cabinets, and securing loose wires and cords. You can also recollect putting in smoke detectors and carbon monoxide detectors to ensure that your own home is safe from capability dangers.

Creating nurturing surroundings on your infant is likewise critical. This way providing them with love, interest, and affection. Spend time playing along with your child, reading to them, and tasty in activities that they revel in. Create a space for your child that is relaxed and inviting, consisting of a playroom or a secure studying corner. It's additionally crucial to offer your baby with a healthful food regimen and encourage them to interact in physical hobby to promote their bodily and intellectual properly-being.

As a accountable determine, it's far vital to be aware about your infant's wishes and to take steps to offer them with the guide and care they want to thrive. By growing a safe and nurturing environment, you can assist your infant broaden the capabilities and self-assurance they want to stand the challenges of growing up.

Remember to have amusing and enjoy the journey

As a discern, it is able to be smooth to get stuck up in the day-to-day responsibilities of raising kids. From changing diapers to scheduling play dates, it is able to feel like there's constantly something that wishes to be carried out. However, it's important to don't forget to take a step back and feature a laugh together with your youngsters.

Whether it's gambling a board game, going on a bike journey, or honestly having a dance celebration in the residing room, taking the time to have fun along with your kids may be a first rate manner to bond with them and create lasting memories. Plus, it could assist to relieve stress and convey a experience of joy and happiness for your day.

Remember, being a responsible figure would not mean sacrificing all sorts of a laugh and enjoyment. In fact, it's important to prioritize a laugh and entertainment on your each day ordinary to preserve a wholesome work-existence balance. So, pass ahead and plan that own family holiday, have that game night time, and experience the adventure of parenthood.

Continuously examine and develop as a discern

Being a accountable determine is an ongoing journey that requires continuous learning and boom. As your infant grows, so have to your parenting capabilities. It's essential to live up-to-date with the latest parenting trends and strategies to make sure you're providing the satisfactory steering and support for your toddler.

One manner to maintain mastering and developing as a determine is to wait parenting classes or workshops. These lessons can offer treasured insights on infant improvement, conduct control, and communication techniques. You also can study books, blogs, and research articles on parenting to advantage new views and strategies for elevating your toddler.

Another manner to study and develop as a determine is to are seeking for feedback from your child. Ask them how they feel about your parenting style and if there's anything you can do to improve. This will not best help you improve as a discern but additionally give a boost to your dating with your child.

Additionally, it's crucial to attend to yourself as a parent. Self-care is vital to preserving your physical and emotional well-being, which, in turn, lets in you to be a higher discern. Take time to practice self-care sports consisting of workout, meditation, or pastimes which you revel in.

In end, being a accountable determine calls for a dedication to non-stop mastering and growth. By staying informed, looking for feedback, and training self-care, you could be the first-class figure possible on your child.

Parenting can be tough, and it is natural to have questions about how to be a accountable parent. We wish our weblog submit provided you with a few practical tips that you may use every day to ensure you're giving your child the high-quality possible upbringing. Remember, there's no one proper manner to be a determine, but by way of following these tips, you will be setting yourself up for fulfillment. Thank you for analyzing, and we wish you all of the nice in your parenting adventure.

ESSENTIAL PARENTING SKILLS FOR RAISING HAPPY AND SUCCESSFUL KIDS

Parenting may be a challenging adventure; however it is also one of the maximum rewarding reports in lifestyles. Every figure wishes their toddler to develop as much as be satisfied, healthy, and successful. However, elevating youngsters in modern day world can be a daunting task. It calls for quite a few patience, dedication, and abilities to nurture and guide your toddler's growth and development. In this publish; we can percentage with you 10 essential parenting abilities to help you enhance glad and a hit youngster. From placing limitations and fostering independence to cultivating empathy and inspiring creativity, these talents will assist you navigate through the u.S.And downs of parenthood and create a loving and supportive surroundings to your child to thrive in.

Communication Skills: Listening and Speaking

Effective communication is prime to a success parenting. This entails each listening and speaking skills. As a parent, it's important to pay attention for your baby's wishes, understand their feelings, and be capable of communicate with them efficaciously. This helps to construct a sturdy courting together with your infant, and it additionally facilitates your toddler to increase sturdy conversation abilities with the intention to serve them well in the course of their lives.

Listening for your baby includes greater than simply listening to what they say. It means actively attractive with them, understanding their attitude, and displaying empathy. This enables your baby to experience heard and understood, which in flip builds their confidence and vanity.

On the alternative hand, speaking successfully on your child includes clean and concise verbal exchange. It's critical to use age-suitable language that your toddler can recognize, and to keep away from using negative or judgmental language. This allows building a nice and trusting courting together with your infant, and it additionally facilitates your toddler to feel valued and revered.

In short, sturdy communiqué capabilities are essential for powerful parenting. By growing your listening and talking skills, you could build a sturdy relationship together with your toddler, assist them to increase strong verbal exchange skills, and in the end increase satisfied and a success youngsters.

Patience and Self-Control

Parenting is a hard process, and it is able to be specially challenging in relation to exercising staying power and self-control. Children may be unpredictable, and their behavior can now and again be frustrating or even infuriating. However, as a determine, it is critical to remain calm and composed with a purpose to model appropriate behavior for your infant.

Practicing patience is important in all elements of parenting. It requires the capability to take a step returned before reacting to a scenario. By doing so, you can assess the scenario and technique it in a peaceful and rational way. This can help to save you arguments and useless conflicts together with your toddler.

Self-manipulate is also an essential parenting talent. It entails being capable of alter your personal emotions and responses to your baby's conduct, even in hard conditions. It's critical for mother and father a good way to hold composure and not allow their feelings dictate their reactions. This can assist to foster a sense of protection and protection in your baby, in addition to constructing a trusting relationship between determine and child.

It's essential to take into account that nobody is best, and parenting may be a consistent getting to know system. However, with the aid of training staying power and self-control, dad and mom can offer their kids with safe and solid surroundings to grow and broaden.

Empathy and Understanding

Empathy and information are two essential competencies that dad and mom need to cultivate in themselves to elevate glad and successful children. Children undergo numerous emotional American downs as they develop up and mother and father want to have the ability to relate to their children's feelings and feelings. Empathy is the capability to position yourself on your toddler's shoes and notice the arena from their angle. When children feel heard and understood, they're much more likely to confide in their parents and percentage their mind and emotions.

It's additionally vital for parents with a view to apprehend their toddler's behavior. Children frequently act out while they're frustrated, tired, or confused. Instead of having irritated or pissed off along with your infant, it's essential to try to apprehend what is causing their conduct. By doing this, you may be capable of reply to your child in a greater compassionate and effective way.

Empathy and know-how also help mother and father build robust emotional connections with their children. When kids experience that their parents recognize their feelings and are there for them, they may be much more likely to feel secure and assured. This feel of safety and self belief is vital for children to thrive and reach lifestyles.

Ultimately, empathy and knowledge are two essential parenting abilities that could help dad and mom improve glad, healthful, and a hit kids. By cultivating these talents, parents can create a extra nice and nurturing environment for his or her youngsters to grow and develop.

Positive Reinforcement and Encouragement

One of the maximum important talents for dad and mom to grasp is positive reinforcement and encouragement. Children need to feel loved and liked, and superb reinforcement allows reinforcing desirable conduct and inspiring effective attitudes.

Praising your infant for their achievements or right behavior will have a profound effect on their self-esteem and self-assurance.

It's important to remember the fact that fine reinforcement does not just imply giving out reward for such things as getting suitable grades or scoring a goal in a sports recreation. It also manner acknowledging smaller achievements and efforts, such as trying their excellent or being kind to others. Encouragement is likewise key in building a toddler's self-assurance and shallowness.

As a determine, it's important to version nice behavior and praise your infant after they exhibit the equal. When your baby sees which you value and appreciate their efforts, they'll be much more likely to preserve to exhibit those behaviors.

It's additionally important to keep away from using bad reinforcement, which include punishment or grievance. While discipline is crucial, it ought to be executed in a constructive way that specializes in coaching and guiding as opposed to punishing. By emphasizing advantageous reinforcement and encouragement, you may create a high quality and supportive surroundings so that it will help your baby grow and thrive.

Setting Boundaries and Consistent Discipline

Setting boundaries and regular discipline are some of the crucial parenting capabilities that could aid in raising glad and successful kids.

Children need to understand what's anticipated of them and what the outcomes are for beside the point conduct. Setting clear boundaries allows youngsters feel secure and recognize what is appropriate and what isn't. It additionally facilitates them broaden willpower, strength of will, and appreciate for others.

Consistent subject is likewise critical. Children need to understand that their moves have consequences and that their dad and mom will continually put into effect the guidelines. This facilitates them develop a experience of responsibility and duty.

When it comes to discipline, it's important to apply high quality reinforcement as well. Praising desirable behavior can be more effective than punishing horrific conduct. Children thrive on nice feedback and being praised for right conduct can inspire them to maintain doing the right component.

However, it is crucial to remember the fact that area should always be age-suitable and by no means abusive. Parents should usually attempt to be calm, company, and fair while disciplining their kids.

Overall, putting barriers and consistent area can help youngsters change into responsible, respectful, and a hit adults.

Flexibility and Adaptability

Flexibility and adaptability are vital parenting abilities that may have a profound impact at the improvement and nicely-being of your infant. Life is unpredictable, and being able to adapt to unexpected situations is a treasured life talent that your baby will carry with them into adulthood.

As a figure, it is important to discover ways to be bendy and modify your parenting style to fit your toddler's converting desires. For example, your infant can be going thru a tough phase wherein they need greater aid and interest. In such instances, it's essential to be bendy together with your time and prioritize your child's wishes.

Similarly, as your child grows older, they may face new demanding situations and situations that require a extraordinary method. It's crucial to be adaptable and willing to exchange your parenting fashion to suit your infant's changing desires.

Being bendy and adaptable additionally means being open to new thoughts and approaches to parenting. It's important to be inclined to examine and try new strategies that assist you to improve a glad and a hit infant.

In end, flexibility and flexibility are essential parenting talents that allow you to increase a resilient and adaptable infant who's equipped to deal with existence's challenges with self-assurance and ease.

Teaching Responsibility and Accountability

Teaching duty and accountability is one of the maximum vital competencies we can impart on our youngsters. It's by no means too early to begin coaching your kids approximately duty and accountability. By doing so, parents can assist their kids come to be greater unbiased, confident and accountable for their moves. This can be accomplished in numerous methods, which include assigning age-suitable chores, encouraging them to take possession of their moves, and coaching them to face the consequences of their movements.

Assigning age-appropriate chores helps children sense like they're contributing to the own family unit and additionally teaches them the importance of duty. This will be as easy as cleansing up their toys, setting the table, or supporting with laundry. As they become old, they are able to tackle extra complicated tasks which include mowing the lawn, cooking meals or even budgeting their allowance.

Encouraging youngsters to take possession in their moves is likewise vital. This manner that they should recognize the results in their actions and take duty for them. For instance, in the event that they ruin a toy, they ought to remember that it's their duty to restore or update it. If they do something wrong, they should own as much as it and make an apology.

Lastly, parents have to educate their children to face the outcomes in their movements. This approach that they must remember the fact that every action has a response, and that they have to be organized to stand the effects in their actions. When kids learn to take obligation for their moves, they emerge as extra accountable and unbiased, which are important abilities for a satisfied and a success existence.

Nurturing Self-Esteem and Confidence

Nurturing self-esteem and self-assurance is one of the maximum important parenting competencies for raising happy and successful children. Children who have a healthful sense of vanity and confidence are better geared up to navigate the challenges of lifestyles and grow to be resilient adults.

One of the excellent ways to nurture shallowness and confidence on your toddler is through positive reinforcement. Praising your toddler for his or her achievements, regardless of how small, can go a long way in building their feel of self-confidence. However, it's critical to ensure that you're praising effort in preference to simply capability. When you reward attempt, you're reinforcing the concept that difficult work and patience are what result in fulfillment, which is a valuable lesson for kids to analyze.

Another manner to nurture shallowness and self-assurance is with the aid of permitting your child to take risks and make mistakes. This may be difficult for some parents, as we obviously want to protect our youngsters from failure and sadness. However, allowing your baby to take risks and make errors allows them construct resilience and learn from their reports. Encourage your baby to try new matters, despite the fact that they might fail, and allow them to know that it is okay to make errors.

Finally, modeling self-esteem and confidence your self is also vital. Your toddler looks up to you as a role model, so if they see you valuing and respecting yourself, they're more likely to do the identical. Show your toddler which you consider in yourself and your abilities, and they may be much more likely to consider in themselves too.

Encouraging Creativity and Problem-Solving

Encouraging creativity and problem-solving is a crucial talent for dad and mom to have when raising glad and hit youngsters. Children who're endorsed to think creatively and clear up problems on their personal grow to be greater assured and self-reliant. They are higher equipped to address demanding situations and setbacks in life, and they are more likely to reach school and past.

As a discern, there are many ways you may encourage creativity and trouble-solving on your baby. Provide them with possibilities to discover and test. Give them access to a ramification of substances, together with art elements, building blocks, and puzzles. Ask open-ended questions that encourage them to think severely and give you their very own solutions to problems. Praise their efforts and inspire them to keep attempting, even supposing they make errors.

It's also important to foster a supportive environment that values creativity and problem-fixing. Show your baby that you recognize their precise ideas and views, and encourage them to percentage their mind and emotions. Celebrate their successes and inspire them to study from their screw ups. By doing so, you may help your child to increase the crucial skills they need to come to be happy and hit adults.

Leading by using Example and Modeling Appropriate Behaviors

Parents preserve a splendid deal of electricity in relation to shaping their kid's behavior. Your children observe and examine from everything you do, so it's vital to lead by instance and model appropriate behaviors for your everyday lifestyles.

Practicing what you pontificate is key to rising happy and a success kids. If you need your children to be respectful, type, and honest, you should exhibit those traits to your personal behavior. Children are much more likely to pay attention for your phrases when they see you lead by instance.

For instance, if you need your children to be physically active and wholesome, then you ought to make sure which you additionally engage in regular workout and wholesome consuming behavior. If you want your kids to be compassionate and empathetic, you then have to make sure that you are also displaying compassion and empathy in the direction of others.

Furthermore, it is crucial to apprehend that kids are continually watching and mastering from you. If you react to situations negatively or take care of stress poorly, your youngsters are more likely to follow healthy. On the opposite hand, if you continue to be calm and manage conditions with a high-quality mind-set, your youngsters are much more likely to do the same.

Overall, modeling suitable behaviors is an important parenting skill which could have a profound effect for your kid's attitudes and behaviors, both now and of their future.

Parenting is a difficult process, and it is easy to feel beaten with the aid of the whole thing you want to do to help your toddler develop and increase. But with the right gear and know-how, you may end up a assured and powerful figure. We wish that the tips we furnished in this newsletter will help you construct robust and fine relationships with your kids and set them up for achievement in life. Remember to love your toddler, spend exceptional time with them, and be affected person with the downs of parenting. Thank you for analyzing and being an extraordinary discern.

RAISING CONFIDENT KIDS: TIPS FOR BUILDING SELF ESTEEM AND RESILIENCE

As mother and father, we need our youngsters to develop up to be confident, resilient, and self-assured individuals. We need them for you to deal with life's challenges with grace and simplicity. However, building vanity and resilience in children isn't always continually clean. The global may be a difficult place, and it's our process to put together our youngsters for it. In this weblog submit, we can explore a few practical pointers and strategies for raising confident, resilient children. From fostering independence and encouraging their passions to promoting a boom mind-set and coaching coping competencies, we're going to cowl all of the bases. With those guidelines, you can help your youngster's increase the vanity and resilience they want to thrive in existence.

Importance of shallowness and resilience in children

Self-esteem and resilience are key elements in helping kids grow to be confident and capable adults. Self-esteem refers to a infant's sense of self confidence, even as resilience is the ability to get better from setbacks and challenges. A child with high shallowness is more likely to be ok with them, take on challenges, and try new things. Similarly, a toddler with resilience is better capable of address strain and adversity, and now not surrenders in the face of setbacks.

When kids have healthful levels of vanity and resilience, they're better ready to deal with the u.S.And downs of lifestyles. They are much more likely to have fine relationships, carry out properly academically, and have a effective outlook on existence. Conversely, kids with low shallowness and resilience may warfare with anxiety, depression, and other intellectual health issues.

As mother and father and caregivers, it's far essential to foster shallowness and resilience in children from an early age. This may be executed by offering safe and supportive surroundings, encouraging children to attempt new things, and praising attempt instead of just fulfillment. By supporting youngsters develop a sense of self confidence and the ability to get better from setbacks; we can set them up for success in all elements of existence.

Signs of low self-esteem and the way it impacts youngsters

Low vanity can manifest in exceptional ways in youngsters. One of the most obvious signs of low vanity is shyness or social withdrawal. Children with low shallowness may also keep away from social conditions or struggle to make buddies. They can also have trouble expressing their mind and emotions, and regularly sense helpless and powerless.

Another sign of low shallowness is terrible self-communicate. Children with low vanity can be overly self-critical and often blame themselves for matters that are not their fault. They may also will be predisposed to examine themselves to others and sense inadequate or inferior.

Low shallowness can also affect a child's educational performance. Children who lack confidence can also struggle with schoolwork and can be hesitant to percentage thoughts or solution questions in class. They may also be fearful of taking dangers and attempting new things, which can restriction their opportunities to study and develop.

It's essential to address low vanity in children as it can have a significant effect on their average nicely-being and future success. Building self-esteem and resilience in kids takes time and effort, but it is well worth it to look your toddler grow right into a assured and successful grownup.

Ways to build shallowness in children

Building vanity in kids is important for their emotional properly-being and usual improvement. As a determine, there are numerous methods you can assist your baby construct self-esteem.

One of the most essential things you could do is to provide your baby with love and affection. This way showing your toddler which you take care of them, through hugging them, announcing "I love you," and taking note of them once they communicate. When kids experience loved, they're more likely to feel good about themselves.

Another way to construct self-esteem is to give your baby opportunities to succeed. This manner setting age-suitable dreams and celebrating once they gain them. Whether it's getting to know to experience a motorbike or getting an amazing grade on a take a look at, acknowledging their efforts and accomplishments will help them feel proud and assured.

Encouraging your baby to strive new things is also important. When youngsters step out of their consolation sector and attempt something new, they research that they may be capable of doing things they never thought they may. This can help construct their self-confidence and shallowness.

Lastly, it's crucial to educate your child how to deal with failure. No one is best, and everybody makes mistakes. Helping your child remember the fact that screw ups and mistakes are a herbal part of lifestyles can assist them increase resilience and get better from setbacks. Encourage them to study from their errors and to preserve trying.

By presenting love and affection, placing manageable desires, encouraging exploration, and teaching resilience, you may assist your baby construct self-esteem and confidence with a view to live with them all through their lives.

Encouraging children to take dangers and strive new matters

It's critical for youngsters to experience assured in themselves and their abilities. One super manner to assist construct this confidence is to encourage them to take dangers and strive new things. This may be whatever from attempting a brand new food to getting to know a new talent or taking over a brand new undertaking.

When children take risks, they analyze to conquer their fears and build resilience. They also research that it is okay to make errors and that failure is a natural part of the getting to know procedure. By encouraging youngsters to take dangers, you may help them expand a boom mind-set, in which they see demanding situations as possibilities to examine and develop, rather than as boundaries to be prevented.

One manner to inspire youngsters to take risks is to offer them with safe and supportive surroundings to do so. This means developing an surroundings in which youngsters feel at ease making errors and wherein they realize they will be supported and encouraged, irrespective of the final results.

You also can model chance-taking conduct to your children. When you're taking dangers and attempt new matters yourself, you show your youngsters that it's k to step out of their comfort sector and that taking risks can cause exquisite rewards.

Overall, encouraging children to take risks and strive new matters is a wonderful manner to construct their confidence and resilience. With your support and encouragement, your children can discover ways to embody challenges and build the talents they want to reach lifestyles.

Praising effort and endurance in preference to simply fulfillment

As mother and father, all of us need our kids to achieve something they do. However, it's miles crucial to understand that success need to now not be the simplest awareness. Praising attempt and staying power will have a high quality effect on constructing self-esteem and resilience in children. It is crucial that we train our children that tough paintings, dedication, and perseverance are critical traits so as to assist them gain their dreams in life.

When youngsters are most effective praised for their fulfillment, they may turn out to be annoying approximately failure, afraid to attempt new things, and absence the resilience to bounce back from setbacks. Praising attempt and staying power, however, encourages kids to take dangers, try new matters, and research from their mistakes. It enables them build a increase mind-set and understand that success is not just about being gifted or clever, however additionally approximately putting in the work.

For instance, in case your child brings home a test with a low grade, in preference to focusing at the grade, reward the attempt they placed into reading and encourage them to preserve operating tough. If they're suffering with a particular difficulty or interest, reward their staying power and willingness to keep trying. This will now not only build their shallowness and resilience, however also their motivation to preserve pushing forward.

In conclusion, praising effort and persistence is a powerful tool in constructing vanity and resilience in children. By focusing on the manner in preference to just the outcome, we can help our kids expand a high quality mind-set towards demanding situations and setbacks, and instill in them the belief that with hard paintings and determination, anything is possible.

Developing positive self-talk and mindfulness

Developing nice self-communicate and mindfulness is an powerful way to construct your toddler's self-esteem and resilience. Positive self-talk is the act of the usage of nice affirmations to counteract bad mind and self-doubt. Encourage your child to exercise high quality self-speak via creating a list of high-quality affirmations that they could recite every day. These affirmations must cognizance on their strengths, abilities, and achievements.

Mindfulness is the exercise of being gift inside the second and aware about your mind and emotions without judgment. This exercise can assist your toddler broaden a more feel of self-focus and emotional regulation. Encourage your child to exercise mindfulness thru activities along with deep respiration, meditation, or yoga.

It's important to model wonderful self-talk and mindfulness to your child. Use superb self-speak while you make errors or encounter challenges, and practice mindfulness in the front of your toddler. This will help them see the price in these practices and lead them to more likely to adopt them.

Remember, constructing self-esteem and resilience takes effort and time. Encourage your child to exercise fine self-communicate and mindfulness consistently, and have a good time their successes alongside the manner. With your guide and steerage, your toddler can broaden a robust feel of self-worth and the ability to conquer demanding situations with self-assurance.

Teaching trouble-fixing abilities and coping mechanisms

Teaching problem-fixing talents and coping mechanisms can help your toddler turn out to be greater resilient and self-assured within the face of challenges. Encourage your infant to take possession in their issues and to technique them as possibilities to learn and grow. Help them understand that it's k to make errors, and that failure is a herbal part of the getting to know system.

One way to do that is to version suitable problem-solving abilities yourself. Talk thru your very own demanding situations and demonstrate the way you approach them with a wonderful and answer-targeted mind-set. When your toddler is struggling with a problem, assist them spoil it down into smaller, more doable components, and brainstorm viable answers collectively. Encourage them to suppose creatively and to consider multiple views.

Another crucial component of teaching coping mechanisms is assisting your child apprehend and manage their feelings. Encourage them to explicit their emotions in healthful methods, which include via journaling, art, or speaking with a trusted grownup. Teach them relaxation strategies, along with deep breathing or mindfulness exercises, which could assist them, control stress and tension.

Finally, it's vital to help your child develop a feel of angle and gratitude. Encourage them to recognition on the high-quality aspects of their life and to be glad about the good stuff they have. This can help them build resilience and hold a fantastic outlook even in hard times. By coaching trouble-solving abilties and coping mechanisms, you could help your child grow to be greater confident, resilient, and better equipped to handle anything challenges come their manner.

Encouraging independence and duty

Encouraging independence and duty in children is a top notch manner to help them construct self-esteem and resilience. When youngsters are given obligations to finish on their own, they feel a sense of feat and satisfaction of their competencies. This can result in accelerated confidence and vanity.

To inspire independence, mother and father need to begin through giving their child age-suitable responsibilities to finish on their own. This may want to include making their mattress, packing their personal lunch, or doing their own laundry. As kids get older, parents can regularly deliver them more duty, including coping with their personal finances or making their very own medical doctor's appointments.

It's vital to remember that mistakes will occur along the manner, and that is okay. Encourage your child to learn from their errors, in preference to residing on them. This will assist them increase resilience and the capability to bounce back from setbacks.

It's also essential to expose your child which you accept as true with them to make their own selections. This can be as easy as permitting them to choose their very own clothes or identifying what to have for dinner. Giving your child autonomy in selection-making can help them increase a experience of independence and self-confidence.

Overall, encouraging independence and responsibility is a amazing way to construct shallowness and resilience in youngsters. By giving them the tools they want to be successful on their very own, you are supporting them broaden a strong sense of self confidence and the capacity to deal with whatever demanding situations come their way.

Creating a secure and supportive surroundings at domestic and college

Creating a secure and supportive environment at domestic and college is vital in constructing shallowness and resilience in kids. Children who feel secure and relaxed are much more likely to take risks, attempt new matters, and expand a tremendous outlook on life.

At home, mother and father can create a secure and nurturing environment through putting clean and consistent boundaries, providing emotional guide, and being attentive to their kid's concerns. This approach growing a domestic where kids feel comfy expressing their emotions, knowing that they may be heard and revered.

In faculty, instructors can create a secure and supportive environment with the aid of selling nice conduct and growing an inclusive and alluring study room. This can consist of encouraging children to work together, praising their efforts, and offering possibilities for them to discover their hobbies and capabilities.

It's critical for each mother and father and instructors to be aware of the impact in their words and movements on kid's self-esteem. Negative comments or complaint may be negative and might erode a child's confidence over time. On the other hand, effective comments and encouragement can assist to construct self-esteem and resilience.

By developing a safe and supportive surroundings at home and college, we will help to build our children's shallowness and resilience, giving them the tools they need to navigate life's challenges with self-assurance and positivity.

Encouraging community involvement and volunteering

Encouraging community involvement and volunteering is a incredible way to assist your baby build shallowness and resilience. When youngsters see the nice effect they can have on others, it may assist them sense correct about themselves and their abilities. Volunteering can also expose youngsters to distinct cultures, existence, and demanding situations that they may now not experience in their ordinary life, assisting them to increase a experience of empathy and understanding for others.

There are many ways to get your child concerned within the network. You can start by using seeking out volunteer opportunities at neighborhood non-income businesses or via organizing a community smooth-up or charity event. You also can inspire your toddler to get involved in faculty clubs or sports that sell network service.

When children volunteer, it is essential to present them age-appropriate obligations and obligations. This will assist them experience like they may be creating a real difference and will supply them a experience of feat. It's also essential to speak for your child approximately why volunteering is important and the way it may benefit both the network and themselves.

Overall, encouraging network involvement and volunteering is a remarkable manner to assist your baby build self-esteem and resilience while additionally creating a tremendous effect on others.

Helping kids broaden a growth mind-set

Helping kids increase a boom attitude is important for constructing their vanity and resilience. A growth mind-set is the perception that abilities, intelligence, and skills can be developed through hard paintings, willpower, and continuous learning. Children with a increase attitude see challenges as opportunities to analyze and grow, as opposed to as threats to their intelligence or self-esteem.

Parents can encourage a increase mindset in their children by using praising their effort and difficult work, in preference to their herbal talents. For example, as opposed to pronouncing, "You are so smart!" say, "I am proud of how hard you labored to learn that new talent!" This facilitates youngsters take into account that their effort and tough work are what cause achievement, in place of innate capabilities.

It's additionally important to teach kids that disasters and errors are a natural a part of the gaining knowledge of method. Encourage them to view disasters as possibilities to learn and develop, in preference to as reasons to surrender. This can be achieved by means of asking questions like, "What did you analyze from this enjoy?" or "How can you use this experience to do better subsequent time?"

Parents can also model a growth mind-set by sharing their very own struggles and disasters, and demonstrating their dedication to non-stop studying and improvement. By modeling a growth mindset, mother and father can assist their youngsters expand the confidence and resilience they want to conquer challenges and acquire their desires.

Conclusion and usual significance of elevating assured children.

In conclusion, elevating assured kids is one of the most essential things a parent can do. Children who're assured and have excessive vanity are higher prepared to deal with the challenges and pressures of every day existence. They are much more likely to take risks and strive new things, and they are less likely to be influenced by using poor peer strain or bullying.

When mother and father cognizance on building their child's shallowness and resilience, they are placing their child up for success in all areas of lifestyles. Confident youngsters are more likely to prevail academically, socially, and professionally.

They are able to form strong relationships and speak efficaciously with others.

It's important to keep in mind that constructing self-assurance is a system that takes time, staying power, and consistency. Parents ought to encourage their kids to strive new matters, provide fantastic reinforcement, and assist them increase a boom mind-set. By doing so, parents can help their youngsters end up assured, resilient, and a hit people.

In cutting-edge society, where self-esteem troubles and tension has become greater common, it is important to make an effort to consciousness on constructing confidence in our children. By doing so, we can assist them emerge as the best variations of themselves and lead glad, satisfying lives.

As dad and mom, it's our job to assist construct our kids' vanity and resilience, and we are hoping that the recommendations and strategies we've provided will help you do simply that. Remember, every toddler is precise and can require exceptional processes, so do not be afraid to test a bit to find what works best in your infant. Building self assurance in your toddler is an ongoing manner, and we want you all of the high-quality as you continue to help your infant's boom and improvement.